T0194326

SERVING God WHOLEHEARTEDLY

REV. BETTY PREMPEH TWIMASI

authorHOUSE®

AuthorHouse™
1663 Liberty Drive
Bloomington, IN 47403
www.authorhouse.com
Phone: 1 (800) 839-8640

Published by AuthorHouse 09/09/2019

ISBN: 978-1-7283-2683-2 (sc)
ISBN: 978-1-7283-2686-3 (hc)
ISBN: 978-1-7283-2682-5 (e)

Library of Congress Control Number: 2019913790

Print information available on the last page.

Any people depicted in stock imagery provided by Getty Images are models, and such images are being used for illustrative purposes only. Certain stock imagery © Getty Images.

This book is printed on acid-free paper.

TABLE OF CONTENTS

And thou shalt love the LORD thy God with all thine heart, and with all thy soul, and with all thy might.

-Deuteronomy 6:5

ACKNOWLEDGEMENT

I would like to thank the Lord Almighty for the grace He has given us for this book. It's by His help that I had the inspiration to write this book, and it's by His help I wrote it.

I would like to thank my brother, Michael Adu-Prempeh for his tremendous support throughout the ministry. God bless you mightily.

Thanks go to my children for their patience, understanding and prayers. Grow in grace dears.

I want to thank Rev. Dr. Kodie for the encouragement, and many thanks also to Apostle E. K. Asamoah for the support he gave me.

My appreciation goes to Rev. Osei Kakari, Rev. Samuel Nana Opoku, Rev. Felicia Gambrah, all the Faithful Ministers Fellowship, Prophetess Abena Rose, Prophetess Marina Dadzie, Apostle &Rev Mrs Nutifafa, Apostle & Mrs. Richard Dumfuor, Rev. Dr. Sylvia Blessing, and all the members of Abundant Life Baptist Church & Resurrection Power Living Bread for your help and training in ministry. To my son in the ministry, Ebenezer Abissath, and Julius Nanor, and to all others who through diverse ways made this a reality, a million thanks to you all.

I would like to thank all my family for great support they have been giving me.

I would like to thank compassion prayer line for the great support and prayers. Dr Rev Issac Anku, Rev Kwaku Agyemang, Bishop Dr Peter Owusu Ansah.Deacon & Mrs Fosu.Dr Rev Darko.Rev Paxman Boadu

Deacon & Mrs Nana Addo

God Bless all the great men and women of God who has supported me throughout my ministry. I couldn't bring all the names God bless you all!

Best for last, I would like to thank my husband, Mr John Domfer Twimasi for his support, encouragement and love. May we have many more beautiful years together.

FOREWORD

To be a Christian is a gift and a blessing from the Sovereign Lord. A gift and a blessing that no man deserved, yet were made possible due to the vicarious death of Christ Jesus on the cross. As Christians, we rejoice in that we are saved by grace through faith in Christ Jesus. We are no longer slaves to sin, neither are we under the tutelage or bondage to the law. We have been taken out of utter darkness of sin and translated to the glorious light of Christ Jesus. Now we can boldly say that we are the children of the Most High God. The Bible declares those who are in Christ are seated with Him in heavenly places. God has brought us into His glorious presence and into an intimate relationship with Himself and our Lord Jesus Christ. To be a Christian is a blessing!

Beloved, such new and blessed life in Christ demands our total devotion to Him who loved us and gave His only begotten Son to do die for our justification (II Corinthians 5:21). As God demanded the Church in the wilderness (Israel) to serve Him wholeheartedly, so the New Testament Church is required by Christ Jesus to do likewise. Jesus emphasized this concept of total devotion to God in Matthew 22:37-38 when He declared, "Thou shalt love the Lord thy God with all thy heart, and with all thy soul, and with all thy mind. This is the first and great commandment." Jesus meant, God must be the only object of our worship, our devotion, and our allegiance. Sadly, some New Testament Christians have taken grace as a license to live anyhow pleasing to them. Yet the Apostle Paul reminds us that grace does not give us the license to sin or to live anyhow, but grace gives us the license not to sin, and the power to serve the Lord wholeheartedly in purity before God.

In this Book, Rev. Betty Prempeh Twimasi draws our attention to our relationship and service to God. Based on Deuteronomy 6:5, "And thou shalt love the Lord thy God with all thine heart, and with all thy soul, and with all thy might," Rev. Betty Twimasi makes a trumpet call to all New Testament Believers to serve God wholeheartedly. She alludes that serving God wholeheartedly demands an absolute humility and obedience to do God's will, without any reservation, and or excuse. She also maintains that Serving God wholeheartedly is our high calling, and we should accept and embraced it for our own good. God demands it, and awaits for our response. Rev. Betty Twimasi, from her many years of ministry in teaching, preaching, and counseling has given several practical tips, and principles that would enhance believers' commitment in serving the Lord God wholeheartedly. She points it out that serving God wholeheartedly does not only mean to fast and pray, but involves family life, marriage life, single life, duties in the Church, and also at the marketplace. She cautions that such service should not be based of feelings or circumstances. To those who are seeking to have an intimate relationship with God, and to serve Him wholeheartedly, "Serving God Wholeheartedly" is the resource you need. Rev. Betty Twimasi has passionately provided step by step principles that would help you in your journey. She points out vividly that such journey of serving God wholeheartedly requires Sincerity, Commitment, Boldness, Persistence, Perseverance, Godliness, Self-Control, Obedience, Prayer, and Holy Spirit Controlled Life. Serving God Wholeheartedly is timely book that needs to be read by all believers. This Book will lift you and usher you to your fullest potential in serving God. The principles presented in the book are excellent resource for pastors, teachers, counselors, Christian therapists, and Christian workers who are burdened to help others enhance their walk with the Lord.

Rev. Isaac M. Arku, Psy.D, Th.D,
Founder & General Overseer
Light of the World Christian Ministries, Intl,
President of Faithful Ministers Fellowship of New York
East Fishkill, New York

INTRODUCTION

In this day and age, it is commonplace to see many Christians struggling in their walk of faith when confronted with problems. Many yet are to come to the point of total surrender to God and the work of the ministry. Christians are called to serve God wholeheartedly in every aspect of their lives, but how do you know when you are serving half-heartedly? How do you know that this particular endeavor requires wholeheartedness? What does it even mean to serve God wholeheartedly? In this blessing of a book, Reverend Betty Prempeh-Twimasi shares practical tips on serving God with all our heart, and what we can do to ensure we continue with diligence throughout our walk with God. Read on and be blessed as you read some topics like;

- What it means to serve God
- Loving God with all your heart, mind and strength
- Serving God through tough times
- Benefits of serving God.

By the time you finish reading this book, you would have gained a treasure of knowledge that will help you in your walk with God, and we pray that as you read and apply these principles, you will be given the strength and grace to serve God wholeheartedly.

CHAPTER ONE

SEEKING THE WILL OF GOD WHOLEHEARTEDLY

Seeking God wholeheartedly is what God desires. Should we serve Him wholeheartedly, we bring His attention to us. This is when we do not grumble in this Christian faith. This will in the long run make you enjoy all of the blessings and the goodies of the Lord in the Land of the Living.

"Lord, I Give It All to You" – A Great Start But Don't Stop There

The above statement is a good example of a prayer of submission, and as we know, submission is absolutely essential to our walk with God. The prayer of submission (and/or dedication) is the beginning step in finding the will of God. The only problem though, most people stop right there. This prayer should not be used as a cover for not knowing His will and not having the desire to continue on to find it. Submission is more than making this consecratory statement and then accepting whatever comes as if it were the will of God. Saying the prayer is easy. Taking the next step and putting forth the time and effort to seek His will is not so easy. Submitting to His will implies that at some time you will find His will. It is one thing to submit to His will in principle, and quite another to seek out the specifics of His will and then carry them out in daily life.

This prayer is NOT meant to say, "Lord, guide me like a rudderless boat and float me to where you want me to be. Amen" This prayer SHOULD end with, "Now that my heartfelt submission has opened the doorway to your heart, mind, and will; I will do whatever it takes to know that will. I will read and study your word, pray and seek your face, and wait in your presence until I hear it. And, once I find out what your will is, I will do it. Amen"

The Bible says that, 'without faith it is impossible to please Him,' and there is no way to grow faith without knowing the will of God. Pleasing God carries an understanding of the importance He puts on asking, seeking, and knocking.

And without faith it is impossible to please {Him,} for he who comes to God must believe that He is and {that} He is a rewarder of those who {diligently} seek Him. – Hebrews 11:6

Salvation is a partnership process. We respond to God by seeking His will. Once we find it, we believe for it. God in turn, accepts our faith and responds with the answer. The prayer of faith is God's vehicle for bringing the fullness of His salvation to man. Faith for each situation is specific because God's will for each situation is specific. Faith depends upon knowing the will of God. This is God's 'Way' – the walk of faith.

"But seek first His kingdom and His righteousness, and all these things will be added to you. Matthew 6:33

Serve God with all you've Got

Rom. 14:12 – So then each of us shall give account of himself to God.

We will all be required to account for everything we do here on earth-days we came late to church, days we were encouraged to work for God but stood back, days we allowed our friends delay us from being on time to church. We are serving God and should therefore not allow men place a lid on the quality of our service to Him. They place a lid when we allow them nag and water down our committed service to God.

Deuteronomy 10:12(NKJV)

12 "And now, Israel, what does the Lord your God require of you, but to fear the Lord your God, to walk in all His ways and to love Him, to serve the Lord your God with all your heart and with all your soul,

Deuteronomy 10:12(MSG)

12-13 – So now Israel, what do you think God expects from you? Just this: Live in his presence in holy reverence, follow the road he sets out for you, love him, serve God, your God, with everything you have in you, obey the commandments and regulations of God that I'm commanding you today— live a good life.

The NCV translation says we should serve God with our whole being, meaning we should serve God with everything we have! Serving God wholeheartedly is serving Him without reservations and excuses. Our service to Him should not be based on our feelings or circumstances. We should serve Him with a determination never to give up.

There is something about wholeheartedness and commitment that paves the way for you. Serving God wholeheartedly shows in your prayer life, in the way you give, in your preparation for service, in the smile on your face, and even your status on blackberry messenger and Facebook. Do not use your soul (seat of your emotion) to serve men but to serve God. When you serve God, He grants you men.

Noticing a weakness in any department in church is a call to service for you. Do not sit down to condemn or criticize.

Mark 12:30(NKJV)

And you shall love the Lord your God with all your heart, with all your soul, with your entire mind, and with all your strength.' This is the first commandment.

Romans 12:1(AMP)

I appeal to you therefore, brethren, and beg of you in view of [all] the mercies of God, to make a decisive dedication of your bodies [presenting all your members and faculties] as a living sacrifice, holy (devoted, consecrated) and well pleasing to God, which is your reasonable (rational, intelligent) service and spiritual worship.

Not serving God wholeheartedly connotes unintelligence on your part. When you understand the word of God, you will quit criticizing unbelievers and begin instead to proclaim God's gospel to them. Do not let the castigation of your friends, roommates and colleagues demoralize you in your service to God. The fact that they castigate you indicates that you are on the right path. Do not envy unbelievers, as envying them puts you on the path to backsliding. As soon as you notice a trace of envy in you for them, call for help!

Nobody can force you to worship God when you know where you are coming from. Ensure that all your daily activities are connected to service-your dressing, eating and sleeping habits should be in service of God. Embracing what God has done for you is the best you can give to.

CHAPTER TWO

WHAT IT MEANS TO SERVE GOD WHOLEHEARTEDLY

The word serving God wholeheartedly may have been used overtime so that we have become quite familiar with it. But what does it mean to serve God wholeheartedly? It is not just in the word but there is another dimension I would like to enlighten you about. The following will help you identify the main connotations behind "serving God wholeheartedly"

1. **Serving God wholeheartedly means serving only God.** (Mathew 4:10, Luke 4:8, Deuteronomy 11:16, Mathew 6:24)

Other gods are not the only idols referred to in this text, your blackberry, money, work, friends, wife and family might take the place of God in your heart.

2. **Serving God wholeheartedly means serving God in sincerity and in truth.** (Joshua 24: 13-15, John 4:24).

Serving God wholeheartedly means serving God in Spirit and in truth. When you are given a responsibility, do not grumble for when you grumble you water down the blessing God has earmarked for you. It is also important that you do not serve God blindly. Let your personality, both mentally and spiritually, be in church to serve Him. Reminiscent of a child learning the numerals, when he knows how to count from 1-50, he is excited but you do not ask him to stop there just because he has learnt a few. Rather, you encourage him to go all the way. It is in this manner that we are expected to serve GOD. You move from one stage to the other.

3. **Serving God wholeheartedly means serving God boldly.** (Daniel 3:16)

Be bold in your service to God. Do not get shy when you are about to preach the gospel. Serving God boldly is best illustrated by the three Hebrew children in the days of Babylon.

Daniel 3:16-17 (MSG)

16-18 Shadrach, Meshach, and Abednego answered King Nebuchadnezzar, "Your threat means nothing to us. If you throw us in the fire, the God we serve can rescue us from your roaring furnace and anything else you might cook up, O king. But even if he doesn't, it wouldn't make a bit of difference, O king. We still wouldn't serve your gods or worship the gold statue you set up."

4. **Serving God wholeheartedly means serving in the pattern of Godliness.** (2 Timothy 1:3, 13, Romans 15:4)

This encompasses learning from the testimonies of our fathers in faith. Lessons should be learnt from illustrations and examples set by our senior pastors and our resident pastors who do admonish us on commitment in our service to God. We shouldn't hear all these as gist, but we should learn from them and ensure we do better than they did in our dedication to the work of God.

5. **Serving God wholeheartedly means serving God consistently.** (Luke 2: 37, Revelations 7:12, 15-16)

We should learn to serve God regardless of the trials and tribulations we might be facing at that point in time in our Christian walk with Christ. Serving God in the most difficult circumstances and situations, including those times when you pray and don't get answers.

When you serve God wholeheartedly there are blessings attached-Col 3:24(NKJV). Ensure you serve God with the whole of your heart for there is a grace for wholehearted service.

Prophetic Declarations

Receive the grace to serve God wholeheartedly. Receive lands you did not labor for in the name of Jesus! Receive cities you did not build; they are becoming yours in the name of Jesus! What you lack most you will have most in the name of Jesus! Amen.

Zechariah 4: 9(NKJV) – "The hands of Zerubbabel have laid the foundation of this temple; his hands shall also finish it. Then you will know that the LORD of hosts has sent me to you.

The hands that lay the foundation shall finish it; no strange woman shall take your place in the house of your husband in the name of Jesus! Amen. You will reap where others have sown in Jesus name! Amen.

CHAPTER THREE

WHEN SERVING GOD, LISTEN TO YOUR HEART

A man's heart reflects the man. Proverbs 27:19 (NIV)

The Bible uses the term "heart" to describe the bundle of desires, hopes, interests, ambitions, dreams, and affections that you have. Your heart represents the source of all your motivations–what you love to do and what you care about most. Even today, we still use the word in this way when we say, "I love you with all my heart." The Bible says what is in your heart is what you really are, not what others think you are, or what circumstances force you to be (Proverbs 27:19). Your heart is the real you. It determines why you say the things you do, why you feel the way you do, and why you act the way you do.

Physically, each of us has a unique heartbeat. Just as we each have unique thumbprints, eye prints, and voiceprints, our hearts beat in slightly different patterns. It's amazing that out of all the billions of people who've ever lived, no one has ever had a heartbeat exactly like yours. In the same way, God has given each of us a unique emotional "heartbeat" that races when we think about the subjects, activities, or circumstances that interest us. We instinctively care about some things and not about others. These are clues to where you should be serving. Another word for heart is passion. There are certain subjects that you feel deeply passionate about and others that you couldn't careless about. Some experiences turn you on and capture your attention, while others turn you off or bore you to tears. These reveal the nature of your heart; listen for inner promptings that can point to the ministry God intends for you to have.

When you were growing up you may have discovered that you were intensely interested in some subjects that no one else in your family cared about. Where did those interests come from? They came from God! God had a purpose in giving you these inborn interests. Your emotional heartbeat is a key to understanding your shape for service. Don't ignore your interests; consider how they might be used for God's glory. There is a reason that you love to do these things. Listen for inner promptings that can point to the ministry God intends for you to have.

Under the leadership of Moses, the people of Israel had completed the long and difficult journey from Egypt to the edge of Canaan. It was finally time to enter and conquer the land God had promised to give them.

Numbers 13 & 14

The Lord said to Moses, "Send some men to explore the land of Canaan. From each ancestral tribe send one of its leaders."

So Moses did as the Lord commanded him. He sent out twelve men, all tribal leaders of Israel, from their camp in the wilderness. One of those twelve men was a man named Caleb, leader of the tribe of Judah. When Moses sent them to explore Canaan, he said, "Look the land over. See what it's like. Assess the people: Are they strong or weak? Are there few or many? Observe the land: Is it pleasant or harsh?

Inspect the cities: Are they unwalled or fortified? Examine the soil: Is it fertile or barren? Are there trees on it or not? Do your best to bring back samples of the fruit of the land." So the twelve spies went up and explored the land. They went as far as Hebron, where the descendants of the giant Anak lived. When they reached the Valley of Eshcol, they cut down a branch bearing a single cluster of grapes that was so large that it took two of them to carry in on a pole between them! After exploring the land for forty days, the men returned to the Israelite camp.

They reported to Moses and the people of Israel what they had seen and showed them the fruit they had taken from the land. Their report was one of good news and bad news. They said, "We entered the land you sent us to explore, and it is indeed a bountiful country—a land flowing with milk and honey! Just look at this fruit! But the people living there are powerful, and their cities are huge and well-fortified.

Worse yet, we even saw giants there—the descendants of Anak! The people began to murmur, but Caleb silenced them. "Let's go at once and take the land," he said. We can certainly conquer it!" Caleb remembered how the Lord had already provided for Israel since they left Egypt— how He had parted the waters of the Red Sea, how He had provided water from a rock, and how He had rained down manna from the sky. Caleb was sure that God would once again help them if they battled against the people of Canaan. But ten of the twelve men who had explored the land with Caleb disagreed. "We can't attack those people; they are stronger that we are." So they spread among the Israelites a bad report about the land. They said, "The land we explored will devour anyone who goes to live there. All the people we saw there are huge. Next to them we felt like grasshoppers, and that's what they thought, too!

The majority measured the giants against their own strength; Caleb measured the giant's against God's strength. The majority trembled; Caleb triumphed. The majority saw great giants and a little God. Caleb saw a great God and little giants.

That night all the people of Israel wept aloud. They grumbled against Moses. They said, "If only we had died in Egypt! Or even here in this desert! Why is the Lord bringing us to this land only to let us fall by the sword? Our wives and children will be carried off as plunder. Wouldn't it be better for us to go back to Egypt?" And they said to each other, "We should choose a new leader and return to Egypt."

Caleb pleaded with the people: "The land we traveled through and explored is a wonderful land! If the Lord is pleased with us, he will bring us safely into that land. It is a rich land flowing with milk and honey. The Lord will give it to us. Only do not rebel against the Him. And don't be afraid of the people of the land. They are helpless prey to us! They have no protection because the Lord is with us. Don't be afraid of them." But the whole assembly began to talk about stoning them. Later, the Lord said to Moses, "As surely as I live, not one of them will ever see the land I promised to their forefathers. No one who has treated me with contempt will ever see it. But because my servant Caleb has a different spirit and follows me wholeheartedly, I will bring him into the land he explored, and his descendants will inherit it." [The above paragraphs are a paraphrase of a few translations (NIV, NLT, The Message) with a few comments thrown in as well.]

Forty-Five Years Later

Let's fast forward forty-five years.

Under the leadership of Joshua, the people of Israel are now in the land of Canaan. They have won many battles and are ready to distribute the land to the twelve tribes of Israel.

Now the men of Judah approached Joshua at Gilgal, and Caleb son of Jephunneh the Kenizzite said to him, "You know that what the LORD said to Moses the man of God at Kadesh Barnea about you and me. I was forty years old when Moses the servant of the LORD sent me from Kadesh Barnea to explore the land and brought him back a report according to my convictions, but my brothers who went up with me made the hearts of the people melt with fear. I, however, followed the LORD my God wholeheartedly. So on that day Moses swore to me, 'The land on which your feet have walked will be your inheritance and that of your children forever, because you have followed the LORD my God wholeheartedly.' "Now then, just as the LORD promised, he has kept me alive for forty-five years since the time he said this to Moses, while Israel moved about in the desert. So here I am today, eighty-five+ years old! I am still as strong today as the day Moses sent me out; I'm just as vigorous to go out to battle now as I was then. Now give me this hill country that the LORD promised me that day. You yourself heard then that the sons of Anak were there and their cities were large and fortified, but, the LORD helping me, I will drive them out just as he said". Then Joshua blessed Caleb son of Jephunneh and gave him Hebron as his inheritance. So Hebron has belonged to Caleb son of Jephunneh the Kenizzite ever since, because he followed the LORD, the God of Israel wholeheartedly. (Joshua 14:6-14).

Six times the Bible says that Caleb followed the Lord "wholeheartedly" (Numbers 14:24; 32:12; Deuteronomy 1:36; Joshua 14:8, 9, 14).

Caleb followed the Lord wholeheartedly because he trusted in the promises of God. When he was forty, he believed God's promise to give Israel the land of Canaan. When he was eighty-five, he believed God's promise to give him and his descendants Hebron.

Mark 12:30 NIV– Love the Lord your God with all your heart and with all your soul and with all your mind and with all your strength.' I would think that if we are told to love the Lord with all our hearts that we ought to pursue its meaning. What does that mean to love God with all our hearts and how do we go about doing it? These are huge questions that need to be clearly answered. The following identifies ways to loving God wholly.

1. Recognize that Our Affections Determine Our Devotion

First, let's determine what the heart is all about. The arena of the heart contains powerful emotions, affections and desires. Our affections are deep currents that steer our lives. Think of them as a rudder of a ship that literally directs it.

To determine where our affections lie, we have to discern what occupies our time, what motivates our actions, and what shapes our aspirations and their rewards. Affections wait to be captured.

They long to cling to someone or something. Wherever these affections are found so our hearts will be.

2. Understand That Our Affections Follow What We Treasure

The devotion of our hearts is determined by wherever we find value as our greatest treasure.

Matt. 6:21 "For where your treasure is, there your heart will also be."

Read this again slowly. "Where your treasure is... your heart will be." I would suggest memorizing this short phrase. Jesus just gave us the answer on how to love God with all our hearts. The heart loves what it treasures! We have to seek a great treasure, and when we discover it, love (the result of our affections) follows. Ironic, isn't it? The treasure comes first, and the heart comes second. Matt. 13:44 *"The kingdom of heaven is like treasure hidden in a field. When a man found it, he hid it again, and then, in his joy, went and sold all he had and bought that field."* In order for the heart to love Jesus completely, it has to treasure Him supremely. Our affections are the outcome of what we treasure. When we truly encounter the Lord in His glory and worth, loving Him with all our hearts will be the end result.

3. **Aim to Make Jesus Your Greatest Treasure**

For the Apostle Paul, Jesus was THE treasure of his life. The loss of everything else was nothing compared to gaining Christ.

Phil. 3:8 NIV "What is more, I consider everything a loss compared to the surpassing greatness of knowing Christ Jesus, my Lord, for whose sake I have lost all things. I consider them rubbish, that I may gain Christ."

Eph. 3:8 AMP "...this grace was given me: to preach to the Gentiles the unsearchable riches of Christ"

Here is a picture of a man who found a treasure that exceeds all others – Jesus. Nothing else comes close! The glory of Jesus is so amazing and so satisfying that once discovered, all else pales in comparison. When we divert our attention away from the Lord, our love will begin to grow cold. It's that simple.

4. Spend Time with The Lord And Let His Light Shine In Your Heart

2 Cor. 4:6-7 For God, who said, "Let light shine out of darkness," made his light shine in our hearts to give us the light of the knowledge of the glory of God in the face of Christ. But we have this treasure in jars of clay to show that this all-surpassing power is from God and not from us.

Only through the persistent gaze on the face of the Lord and His glory do the streams of light pierce our hearts with the same power and force that keep the Seraphim consumed before His throne (Rev. 4:8).

Initial Steps to Consider

We have to decide to pursue Him. Just pray it to the Lord: "Jesus, I long for You to be my ultimate treasure. Help me and give me power to do so!" Pray this often throughout the day. Let the Lord know that you have a deep and longing desire to have Him. Paul said he considered everything a waste, just so he could have Christ. Start with the Bible. Open it and search out what it says about the glory of who Jesus is and what He has done. If you don't know where to start, just go to the Gospels. Study the life and ministry of Jesus. Read about his love for you and the sacrifice he has made for you. Make adjustments. What is it you are going to do daily that will allow you to grow into this reality? Write it down. Schedule it. Be with Him. He delights in you. He wants to be with you and reveal Himself to you. He enjoys you! Set time aside to be with Him only.

We must continue to stand firm in the Lord no matter what the situation is. We must continue to love Lord in all our ways always.

CHAPTER FOUR

WHOLE-HEARTED, LIFE-ENCOMPASSING ALLEGIANCE TO GOD

So are we on target reading it this way? The context of this passage would suggest we are. Deuteronomy 6:6–9 stress that treasuring God's oneness and uniqueness needs to be personally applied to our lives (Deuteronomy 6:6, 8). It needs to impact relationships (Deuteronomy 6:7), and what goes on at home and in the work place (Deuteronomy 6:9).

"The Bible calls us to wholehearted, life-encompassing, community-impacting, exclusive commitment to our God."

This means that the covenant love we're called to must be wholehearted, life-encompassing, community-impacting, exclusive commitment to our God. And this God is our God only because he has now revealed himself to us in the person of his Son. This kind of love we should have for him doesn't exist apart from love for Jesus — for Jesus and the Father are one (John 10:30).

This truth means that every closet of our lives needs to be opened for cleaning, and every relationship in our lives must be influenced. This call to love God this way destroys any option of being one person at church and another person on a date. What you do on the internet needs to be just as pure as what you do in Bible-reading. The way we talk to our parents needs to be as wholesome as the way we talk to our pastors.

There needs to be an authentic love for God that starts with God-oriented affections, desires, and thoughts, that permeates our speaking and behavior, and then influences the way we spend our money and how we dress, and drive, and our forms of entertainment. Whether we're eating or singing, jogging or blogging, texting or drawing, love for Yahweh — the one true triune God — is to be in action and seen.

What does it mean to Love God with All?

Mark 12:30 CPDV says, "And you shall love the Lord your God from your whole heart and from your whole soul and from your whole mind and from your whole strength."

Briefly speaking, this verse means that God wants us to love Him with our whole being.

So what is our whole being?

In studying the Difference between the Soul and the Spirit, 1 Thessalonians 5:23 shows us all three parts of our being, saying, "And the God of peace Himself sanctify you wholly, and may your spirit and soul and body be preserved complete, without blame, at the coming of our Lord Jesus Christ."

Our spirit is the innermost part of our being, the part we use to receive God and contact Him. When we received the Lord Jesus as our Savior, this is where He came to live in us. In our spirit we can have fellowship with the Lord and spend time in His presence.

Our soul is made up of our mind, our emotion, and our will. It is our person, our psychological part. When you want to make a decision, it is your soul that you use to make the decision. The nature of the soul can change, in that your values, beliefs and convictions can change based upon what you give the soul.

Our body, of course, is our physical part, with which we contact physical things through our five senses and express our inward parts. It involves all our physical efforts and may include, in biblical terms, the fruit of your labour.

The Lord Jesus said that we are to love God with these three parts, that is, with our whole being. This is a strong yet mysterious commandment. First Peter 1:8 says, "Whom having not seen, you love; into whom though not seeing Him at present, yet believing, you exult with joy that is unspeakable and full of glory." How can we love someone we haven't even seen? And how do we love God with our whole heart, our whole soul, our whole mind, and our whole strength? Do we even have this ability?

Let's take a look at how we love God wholly and absolutely with each of the parts of our being.

It all begins with our heart.

We may think of our heart simply as the seat of our emotions. But in the Bible our heart is more than that; it's composed of our emotions, yes, but also of our mind, our will, and our conscience. Our heart is the source of our feelings, thoughts, intentions, and our sense of condemnation or guilt when we've done something wrong.

God created us with a heart so that we would love Him wholly and absolutely. Today, however, our hearts love many things besides God. We would find it difficult to pray with the psalmist, "Whom do I have in heaven but You? And besides You there is nothing I desire on earth" (Psa. 73:25). We must admit that though we may love God to some extent, He is not our only, or our first love sometimes. The things of the world tug at our heart. So how can we obey the Lord's command to "love the Lord your God from your whole heart"? First John 4:19 says, "We love because He first loved us." The note on this verse in the New Testament Recovery Version says, "God first loved us in that He infused us with His love and generated within us the love with which we love Him and the brothers (vv. 20-21)." God commanded us to love Him absolutely, but He never intended us to work up this love for Him out of our own effort. In fact, He is well aware that we, in ourselves, aren't even capable of such love. We need to realize that when God makes a demand, His intention is that He Himself would come to meet that demand for us. Our love for God actually originates from God Himself.

It comes from His love within us, which is higher than anything we can generate. God is love, and He became a man named Jesus Christ. When we receive the Lord Jesus, we receive all that He is into our spirit. The good news for us Christians is that we can turn our hearts to Him where He is in our spirit. Second Corinthians 3:16 says, "Whenever their heart turns to the Lord, the veil is taken away." Then verse 18 says, "But we all with unveiled face, beholding and reflecting like a mirror the glory of the Lord, are being transformed into the same image from glory to glory, even as from the Lord Spirit." These verses liken human beings to mirrors that reflect what they behold. When our heart is turned away from the Lord by things such as sins, preoccupations, and love for worldly things, our heart is covered by a veil, and we can't see or reflect the Lord. But when we turn our heart to the Lord within us, the veil is removed, and we can see the glorious Christ. We see His beauty, His virtues, and how wonderful He is, and He imparts what He is, including love, into us. Our love for Him grows.

We can turn our hearts to the Lord Jesus by praying to Him, calling on His name, confessing to Him and applying His precious blood, and spending time in His Word. These simple practices can remove the veils from our heart, restore our fellowship with the Lord, and rekindle our love for Him. We don't have to remain in coldness or indifference toward God. We can turn our heart to Him at any time. He will revive us and bring us back to Himself as our first love.

Our Soul

Our soul—our mind, emotion, and will—is a large part of our heart. God created our soul so we could express Him, but because of the fall, we tend to express ourselves. We have our own opinions, our own feelings, and our own decisions apart from God.

But when we turn our hearts to the Lord, our love for Him grows. We love Him with our heart, and, specifically, we begin to love Him with our soul. His thoughts become our thoughts, His feelings become our feelings, and His decisions become our decisions. As He does His transforming work in us, we spontaneously express God and glorify Him. Others see Christ expressed in us by our loving Him with our whole soul.

Our Mind

Our mind is the leading part of our soul, directing the rest of our being. It can be set on many things, but God wants it to be set on the spirit, where Christ is. Romans 8:6 says, "For the mind set on the flesh is death, but the mind set on the spirit is life and peace." When we set our mind on the flesh or fleshly things, we feel lifeless and uneasy because we're turned away from Christ in our spirit. But when we set our mind on our spirit, we're peaceful and full of life. By setting our mind on our spirit, our whole being is focused on God. One way to set our mind on the spirit is to read the Bible with an open heart. As we read, our mind is enlightened and renewed, and we are washed by the water in the Word. Reading God's Word daily greatly benefits our mind and our entire soul.

Our Strength

Our strength refers to our physical strength. When we turn our heart to the Lord, express Him in our soul, and set our mind on Him, our body will follow. We formerly used our strength to serve ourselves or the world, but as love for the Lord pervades all our inward parts, our outward actions will begin to change. Things that used to occupy our time and energy will give way because what we love has changed. We have a new aim, a new goal, and a new pursuit. Our physical strength is now for His purpose.

Start Today

To love God with our whole being is an exercise. We don't always wake up in the morning with a loving heart toward the Lord. But we can start the day by turning our hearts to our dear Lord Jesus. We can say, "Lord Jesus, I turn my heart to You this morning. I love You!" We can practice telling the Lord we love Him every single day. We can also pray, "Lord Jesus, cause me to love You more today than I did yesterday." As we pray back to our Lord His own desire for us to love Him absolutely, He will have the way to work Himself into us so that we love Him with our whole being!

The Lord asks us to serve with all of our heart, might, mind, and strength. It is a sacred privilege to serve God. It is our hope that this year and in the years to come each of us will learn to serve with greater commitment in the way the Savior has instructed — with all our heart, might, mind, and strength. How can we do that? Here are some ideas. "As you serve God with your whole soul, He promises that you will be cleansed from sin and prepared to stand before Him." First, we serve with all of our hearts. We understand this to mean that your service to God must be motivated by your love for Him and His children. "Our love of the Lord will govern the claims for our affection, the demands on our time, the interests we pursue, and the order of our priorities" "The Great Commandment—Love the Lord," You show the Lord your love when you keep His commandments You serve in your home and strengthen your family. You magnify your calling and reach out to those who need a friend. You find family names to take to the temple.

Second, we serve with all of our might. Physical labor and diligent effort are required. Missionary work requires stamina and endurance. You serve with might when you attend to the needs of others, "such as feeding the hungry, clothing the naked, visiting the sick and administering to their relief, both spiritually and temporally"

Next, we serve with all of our mind. Your thoughts must be clean and pure, centered on the Savior. You have covenanted to always remember Him. You seek the guidance of the Holy Ghost through scripture study and prayer. As you align your thoughts, words, and actions with the mind and will of God, you recognize the needs of others and are worthy and ready to serve.

Finally, we serve God with all of our strength. One way to obtain strength is to exercise faith in the Savior's Atonement. You repent and sanctify yourself through obedience to His commandments. You feel the Savior's enabling power and witness miracles as you serve in the strength of the Lord.

Love God with Your Everything
Loving with All Our Heart

Love. There are few things so universal and yet so challenging. Love for God. "The most important" commandment, says Jesus (Mark 12:29–30), and one that both the old and new covenants portray as necessary to enjoy God's sustained favor. As Moses asserted, Yahweh "keeps covenant and steadfast love with those who love him and keep his commandments, to a thousand generations," but he "repays to their face those who hate him, by destroying them." (Deuteronomy 7:9–10) Similarly, Paul declared that "all things work together for good" only for "those who love God . . . who are called according to his purpose" (Romans 8:28).

Some have tagged the Supreme Command of Deuteronomy 6:5 the "all-command," because of the three-fold "all" — "You shall love the Lord your God with all your heart and with all your soul and with all your might" (ESV). There is no room here for divided affections or allegiance. As Jesus said, "No one can serve two masters" (Matthew 6:24). If indeed there is one God who stands supremely powerful and valuable (Deuteronomy 6:4), this demands a supreme and total loyalty from you and me, a loyalty that starts with the heart.

While surprising to some, the old covenant recognized that a spiritual relationship with God begins from within, with a proper disposition toward the preeminent Savior, sovereign, and satisfier. From the heart "flow the springs of life" (Proverbs 4:23), and without one's will, desires, passions, affections, perceptions, and thoughts rightly aligned, the life of love is impossible.

Therefore Moses calls Israel to "know... in your heart" that God disciplines like a father his son (Deuteronomy 8:5). He urges God's people to "lay it to heart" that there is no God besides Yahweh (Deuteronomy 4:39–40) and to ensure that his words "be on your heart" (Deuteronomy 6:6), thus anticipating the miraculous heart-work that the new covenant would realize (Jeremiah 31:33).

Loving With All Our Soul

Along with our hearts, we are called to love Yahweh with all our soul. In the first five books of the Old Testament the "soul" refers to one's whole being as a living person, which includes one's "heart," but is so much more. For example, in Genesis 2:7 we are told that "Yahweh God formed the man of dust from the ground and breathed into his nostrils the breath of life, and the man became a living [soul] creature" (Genesis 9:5).

Elsewhere, corpses are called "dead souls," which simply means the person, once alive, is now dead (Leviticus 21:11), and Yahweh promises that his "soul [i.e., his being] shall not abhor" all who follow his lead (Leviticus 26:11). In light of these texts, it seems Moses starts with a call to love God from within and then moves one step larger saying that everything about us as a person is to declare Yahweh as Lord.

So we are to love God with our passions, hungers, perceptions, and thoughts. But we are also to love him with how we talk, and what we do with our hands, and how we utilize our talents, and how we react to challenges — our entire being is to display that we love God.

Loving With All Our Might

What then is the meaning of loving God with our "might"? The word translated "might/strength" in Deuteronomy 6:5 usually functions as the adverb "very" in the Old Testament (298x). The noun version occurs in Deuteronomy and in only one other place, which itself is just an echo of our passage. In 2 Kings 23:25 we are told that King Josiah "turned to Yahweh with all his heart and with all his soul and with all his might."

So if the word usually means "very," what would it mean to love the Lord will all our "very-ness"? Interestingly, the Greek translation of this word is "power." The Aramaic translation is "wealth." Both of these may actually be pointing in the same direction, for the strength of a person is not simply who he is, but what he has at his disposal. Think with me: If Moses's call to love Yahweh starts with our heart and then moves out to our being, could not our "very-ness" be one step bigger and include all our resources.

This means that the call to love God is not only with our physical muscle, but with everything we have available for honoring Him. As you serve God with your whole soul, He promises that you will be cleansed from sin and prepared to stand before Him and receive His eternal glory. There are also benefits unspeakable that we would enjoy in the journey of faith with the Father.

CHAPTER FIVE

SERVING GOD THROUGHOUT YOUR JOURNEY

Rom. 8:38, 39 KJV– For I am persuaded, that neither death, nor life, nor angels, nor principalities, nor powers, nor things present, nor things to come, nor height, nor depth, nor any other creature, shall be able to separate us from the love of God, which is in Christ Jesus our Lord.

Paul was a great minister of the gospel, and a role model to just about every evangelist and preacher in Christendom. He wrote 13 letters which served as a guide to many Christians, and still does in our time as well. He wrote this excerpt in his letter to the Romans, which was a declaration that nothing will separate him from the love of God. He didn't state that it won't stop God's love for him, it just stated that it won't separate him from the love of God. That includes love for God as well as God's love for him.

If God has stated that nothing will change his love for us, why should we allow something to change or affect our love for God and service to God? When we start to embark on any kind of trip, we find that we prepare to the best of our ability, in order to ensure a smooth journey. We prepare in terms of the physical and psychological aspect of the journey, reminding ourselves of the realities of petrol refills, tiredness, hunger and the likes. We also ideally prepare for flat tires, documents for the police and arrangements for where we will stay when we reach our destination. In our Christian walk, we similarly prepare for the journey.

We know that all things work for good for those who love the Lord, but the Bible – even in the words of Jesus – makes us understand that certain "unexpecteds" may come our way and we will need to continue to serve God in spite of all the challenges we face during our journey. Does a traveler terminate his journey because he had a flat? Does a traveler terminate his journey because he was tired? Does a traveler terminate his journey because the destination seemed so far, or because people ridiculed him, or because he ran short of funds? No! He pushes on and perseveres because his eye is on the destination, not the journey.

In my own life, I have been at points where I had overwhelming reasons to give up on this journey. In my own journey throughout ministry, it has involved money, involved strength, and involved time, but as I had made up my mind and surrendered to God, nothing was pushing me down. Even when there were storms, and even when adverse situations arose, I still raised up my head to my King. I said "It's you who has called me, so strengthen me so that nothing can push me down." It's important for Christians, as children of God, as ministers, as deacons and deaconesses, and elders to know that sacrifice is very important, and that's what God wants. It's all about the heart; because if the heart refuses or rejects to serve God, it will be virtually impossible to do what you want to do for the Kingdom, and for you to move forward in ministry and in your Christian journey. During my mission I was going from town to town, and even though things were tough I pushed through. Sometimes you get to a point when you don't have anything on you, but you still have to go and preach, teach and help the people that are in need. But without the heart accepting this situation – that it's God who will do it, not man – you cannot go on.

So serving the Lord throughout the Mission that he has ordained for you is very important. Christians must rise and shine throughout the mission time, because if you do not go out there you cannot win. If you don't go out there you cannot impart. If you do not go out there you cannot help. Hold on and hang on, and know that our Christian faith will be culminated when we get to Paradise to meet our maker.

Get Alone with God!
Understanding the Power of Solitude

In your service to God, you can learn from the Principles of Leadership. Leaders understand the value of solitude. Leaders spend lots of time alone away from the noise and bustle of everyone and everything else. They spend time alone to strategize, reflect and plan. Everyone is always so busy and they don't take time to think, but leaders know that planning and strategizing alone is as important as making and taking decisions with others. This principle can be used in our Christian lives.

Most of us don't like to be alone. We are used to constant conversation and companionship. We are used to the noise.

Be honest, even when you are in the car alone, you can't stand it and you turn on the radio. Teens post on the FB page, "Bored, it's been over 5 minutes since I heard from anyone... htc [hit the cell!]" If you are at home alone the TV has to be on, even if you are vacuuming and cannot possibly hear it! And if your computer dies or the power goes off, then maybe you'll talk to God, you know, since there's nothing better to do.

But leaders understand that times of quiet are vital in life. In the quiet we receive a clear vision from God. He wants to speak to us if He can get a word in edgewise. He WILL speak to us if He can cut through the noise! Nehemiah needed 3 days to hear from God. Before he begins the work he wants to pause and make sure he does it God's way, not his own way. Otherwise he will be wasting time and money. Some would look at him and say, what a waste of time; he could have been 3 days down the road on this project. But it is never a waste of time to get alone with God! Later it was proven that Nehemiah was miles ahead... because of the time he sat still! This multi-year project was accomplished in 52 days... unbelievable!

"Time spent in prayer and planning is always recovered in performance." So don't rush into your day, take time to pray.

Read and enjoy this poem. It should encourage you to spend more time in prayer before starting your day.

I got up early one morning,
And rushed right into the day;
I had so much to accomplish,
I didn't have time to pray.

Troubles just tumbled about me,
And heavier came each task.
"Why doesn't God help me?" I wondered.
He answered, "You didn't ask."

I tried to come into God's presence;
I used all my keys at the lock.
God gently and lovingly chided,
"Why, child, you didn't knock.

I wanted to see joy and beauty,
But the day toiled on gray and bleak.
I wondered why God didn't show me.
He said, "You didn't seek."

So I woke up early this morning,
And paused before entering the day.
I had so much to accomplish
That I had to take time to pray.

-By Regine Anne Baldomar

You can't out give God. Give Him time each day and He'll give you more back. Give Him 3 services a week and you'll have more free time than those who lay out of church!

Consider this illustration as portrayed in the Bible. Elijah found himself discouraged, needing God. He got alone with God on a high mountain. It was there that he heard a mighty wind. But God was not in the wind. And a great earthquake rumbled with powerful noise. But God was not in the earthquake. Then a fierce fire swept through. But God was not in the fire. And then there came a still small voice... it was the voice of God! In the quiet we receive the power of God.

Isaiah 40:31 KJV

31 But they that wait upon the LORD shall renew their strength; they shall mount up with wings as eagles; they shall run, and not be weary; and they shall walk, and not faint.

Nehemiah knew this undertaking was impossible without the power of God. And at our various churches I think we've seen what we can do, but I'm thirsty to see what God can do!

How did Moses prepare for his ministry? 40 years alone in the desert!

How did the Apostle Paul prepare? 3 years in the Arabian Desert! He entered the desert with a knapsack and came out with the book of Romans!

Jesus spent 40 days in solitude in the wilderness fasting and praying to defeat the devil and yield not to His temptations. If Christ needed solitude, how much more do you and I?

Mark 1:35 KJV

And in the morning, rising up a great while before day, he went out, and departed into a solitary place, and there prayed.

Luke 4:42 KJV

42 And when it was day, he departed and went into a desert place:

Luke 5:16 KJV

16 And he withdrew himself into the wilderness, and prayed.

Matthew 14:22, 23 KJV

And straightway Jesus constrained his disciples to get into a ship, and to go before him unto the other side, while he sent the multitudes away. And when he had sent the multitudes away, he went up into a mountain apart to pray: and when the evening was come, he was there alone.

CHAPTER SIX

FIVE PEOPLE WHO SERVED GOD
WITH ALL THEIR HEARTS

All throughout the Bible, we are shown examples of people who served God wholeheartedly and at the end, they were blessed beyond expectation. God is a rewarder of them that diligently seek Him. All these people, and more, went through periods of adversity but the still put their faith in God, deciding to still serve Him in spite of the challenges. These were written to provide encouragement to us in these last days, giving us examples to look up to. Let's take a brief look at the following personalities and "heroes" of the Faith.

Joseph

Sold by his brothers because of jealousy, Joseph found himself in a strange land. He had received a vision from God that showed that he was going to be great, but here he was – a slave in a foreign land. Joseph could have decided to quit on God when things weren't going according to expectation. "How will I rule as a slave?" he may have asked. In spite of all this, he still held on to his principles and faith in God, knowing that God is with him. When Potiphar's wife offered him free carnal pleasure, he fled from the sin she was offering, still having faith in a God who seemed lost in this foreign land. In prison, Joseph still held on to his faith, serving God by being kind and responsible in the prison. We all know that these were events that preceded his ascension to the Second in Command in Egypt. Had he given in to the woman's advances, the chain reaction would never have taken place that led to the salvation of Israel.

You may find yourself in a position that allows you to take advantage of others or of the system, to the detriment of your Christian life and service. Are you taking advantage of your spouse's benevolence and love and therefore taking them for granted? Are you taking of your friend's gadgets and technology to waste time doing unprofitable things? Are you treating your employees or employer with contempt or disdain? Does your life portray the love of Christ or the love you have for yourself? Make sure that all that you do pleases and glorifies God. Remember that when asked, Jesus said the second greatest commandment is to love your neighbor. Loving God will require an element of loving your neighbor. Hold on and choose to serve God wholeheartedly in spite of persecution.

Esther

Esther was living in a time where her people were under foreign rule. Due to the mistake of Queen Vashti, Esther now found herself in a position of power. At the beginning, however, she concealed her identity.

As Christians, we ought to know when to reveal our talents, gifts and identity. We must never hide our identity as Christians or as children of God, but we don't have to toot our horns when we get some form of resource. Esther could have taken advantage of her position and imposed her power over the Jews, or even the Persians who probably were maltreating the Jews. She could also have immediately used her position to make life easier for the Jews, but that would most likely have given Haman more leverage against the people of Israel. We need to know when to use the position God has given us for good. This can be done when we serve God wholeheartedly and when we trust God with our whole heart.

When the time finally came for Esther to reveal her identity in order to save her people from the plot Haman had devised to destroy them, she did so only after she had fasted and prayed to God. After that, she went to the King, which was against the law. And she resolved to fast and then go, being prepared to lay down her life.

*Esther 4:11 KJV– All the king's servants, and the people of the king's provinces, do know, that **whosoever**, whether man or woman, shall come unto the king into the inner court, **who is not called, there is one law of his to put him to death,** except such to whom the king shall hold out the golden sceptre, that he may live: but I have not been called to come in unto the king these thirty days.*

*Esther 4:16 KJV– Go, gather together all the Jews that are present in Shushan, and fast ye for me, and neither eat nor drink three days, night or day: **I also and my maidens will fast likewise; and so will I go in unto the king, which is not according to the law: <u>and if I perish, I perish</u>.***

Child of God, are you prepared to die for the people God has entrusted in your care? Are you prepared to do whatever it takes to keep them safe from the plans and machinations of the enemy? Are you doing it in the will of God and according to the leading of the Holy Spirit? Esther served God with her whole heart, and it led to the salvation of the Jews.

Paul

Paul is by far one of the greatest inspirations in the New Testament. He was a man that was so devoted to God, so led by the Spirit of God, and so loving and caring towards the children of God. Paul wrote many letters to churches that were established either directly by him, or by people who had heard of the gospel through his many spiritual children. And even though all throughout the Bible we are told of Paul's zeal, he didn't start on the right side of the equation.

Paul started off as a persecutor of the Church of Jesus Christ. The first time we encounter him – then called Paul – he was watching over the cloaks of people who were stoning a preacher of Christ. Then we learn that He is seriously opposed to the 'blasphemous' message of salvation that the Christians were professing. On his way to carry out arrests and executions, he meets the resurrected Christ, who calls him to preach to the Gentiles.

Saul, whose name is changed to Paul, goes out to preach the Gospel he so vehemently condemned with the same, if not more, passion and zeal. He lived his life for Christ and ultimately died in his service to God. He summarized his Christian life in these words...

2 Timothy 4:6-7 KJV– For I am now ready to be offered, and the time of my departure is at hand. I have fought a good fight, I have finished my course, I have kept the faith:

Knowing with full confidence that his demise was a passing on to greater glory, he was fine with death and exhorted Timothy to continue his ministry with zeal and passion.

Paul's life should inspire us to do our best in our service to God, serving him wholeheartedly and without hesitation, even when our lives are in peril due to persecution. In the song I Pledge Allegiance to the Lamb by Ray Boltz, these profound words are spoken in the introduction;

...they could choose to live this one life here on earth and reject Jesus and be damned, or they could choose to believe in the words of Jesus and live forever.

We have a choice to make here on earth, and a heart that loves the Lord with their all will always make the right choice.

Job

Job. Who else in the whole of Scripture went through a fraction of what he went through? Let me try and translate it into today's society.

Imagine you have 7 sons, 3 daughters, 3,000 commercial vehicles, 500 employees, 500 retail stores, and a very great household – servants, pool and all – such that you are the greatest person in your global region. Then all of a sudden you lose it all… children die, businesses collapse, employees are lost to other businesses, houses are lost and you are only left with your wife. All this happens even though you remain faithful to God and remain in devoted service to the Most High. What would you do?

Many may desert God, expecting Him to at least protect you because of your service to Him. But wholehearted service says "God, I am with you even when things are not going well, because I know you are with me."

Job was advised to curse God and just die, after he had lost the remaining health he had on him. He could have given in to his friends who suggested that he must have committed some atrocity to warrant this treatment he was receiving. He defended himself and his innocence until finally, God came and spoke some sense into his head. As Christians we must understand that God is with us no matter what, and we ought to keep in mind that His love for us will not allow us go into situations beyond us. HE said there will be a way of escape. Hold on, child of God!

Jesus

Who in the history of the world demonstrated more wholeheartedness to God than our Lord and Saviour, Jesus Christ? The Bible says he remained "faithful unto death". Jesus Christ was a divine person who had the power to command angels, multiply fish, raise the dead, have spiritual meetings, rebuke the teachers of the Law, work on the Sabbath, lay down his life and take it up again. Despite his divine nature and power, he chose to die a painful and shameful death on the Cross for you and I. Paraphrasing Romans 5:7&8, "human beings will hardly die for even a righteous man, but maybe it is possible that someone will dare to die for a good man. But God showed us great love because while we were still living in great sin, Christ died for us".

What love and devotion! Jesus Christ provides us with a great example in wholehearted service to God. Will you preach the Gospel to the guy at your workplace who behaves unfriendly towards you? Will you preach the gospel to your roommate who is dating and fornicating with multiple partners? Will you preach the gospel to the tavern frequenter? Will you demonstrate the love of God to the people in your area and environments? Look unto to Jesus, the author and finisher of our Faith and the one who enables us serve with all our strength, heart and might.

There are more personalities in the Bible who exhibited great tenacity and devotion and these put them on a pedestal we can look up to. Let's follow these positive examples that were given by God's servants. There will be times when we go through similar problems and we can get encouragement from the Word of God.

Serve The Lord Gladly

Romans 12:11

As a response to God's mercies through Christ detailed in the first eleven chapters of Paul's letter to the Romans, Paul calls for all believers to present their bodies to God's service as well as their souls to God's transformation. Paul urges all believers to resist the world's attempt to cram them into its way of doing things and open their life to continual transformation as a result of renewed thinking. The rest of Paul's letter then details some vital areas where we must think right if we are to constantly live right. Renewed thinking always precedes consistent transformed living. God gave us the Scriptures for our transformation not just for our information.

All Scripture is inspired by God and profitable for teaching, for reproof, for correction, for training in righteousness; so that the man of God may be adequate, equipped for every good work. 2 Tim. 3:16-17 NASB

I. God's true disciples not only hear but heed His word. Blessing and stability come from those who hear and heed.

II. Receive God's gift of righteousness 1-5

III. Apply God's gift of righteousness 6-8

IV. Understand God's gift of righteousness in relations to Israel 9-11

V. Live God's gift of righteousness 12-15

A. Get your thinking and living straight – 12:1-2

1. Dedicate your bodies completely to God
2. Dedicate your soul to transformation by constant renewed thinking

So far, Paul's letter has addressed several areas where our thinking needs to be renewed so our living can be transformed

B. Think and live responsibility concerning the body – 12:3-8

1. Realize the general design of the body 3-5
2. Exercise your specific gifting 6-8
3. Show genuine love for one another 12:10

   a) Abhorring what is evil
   b) Clinging to what is good
   c) Loving one another with brotherly love of a family member
   d) Outdoing one another in honor

C. Think and live in diligent service for God – 12:11

Here Paul zeros in on the central focus of life and love; its pattern, its power and its purpose

Regarding diligence – not lazy (The pattern)

Regarding the Holy Spirit – boiling, on fire (The power)

Paul encouraged a fervent, passionate service to the Lord energized by the Holy Spirit. Within every genuine Christian resides a nuclear energy source in the Holy Spirit. It is actually better than that because the indwelling Holy Spirit is a real person who feels and cares and is committed to come along side every believer just as Jesus walked beside and encouraged His disciples. Jesus promised "another" comforter or encourager like Him in the Holy Spirit. His presence brings whatever power necessary to carry out God's specific directives for each person. He is your personal perpetual pastor to encourage and empower you in your spiritual walk. By an act of our will, we seek the continual fullness of the Spirit's work in our life. In our seeking, in our searching, in our longing, we discover the things that block His life-giving river from flowing in and through us. In our seeking we also discover the things in our life that grieve Him. In our seeking we realize how we quench Him through disobedience and unbelief. The children of Israel did not enter into the fullness of God's promised rest because of unbelief. We must first understand what he has promised to do and how we block His work in our life by our willful sin and unbelief. Then, by an act of faith we knock on heaven's door with expectant heart and full assurance that God will do in and through us what we ourselves cannot do. Then, with a heart full of faith, we cry out to God and ask for His blessing and His fullness to actually manifest in and through our life. Seek and you will find. Knock and the door will be opened Ask and it shall be given. As individuals and as a church let us continue to seek, knock and ask for the fullness of God's power to flow in and through us.

CHAPTER SEVEN

STEPS TO LOVING GOD WHOLEHEARTEDLY

1. We can love God by keeping God's commandments. This one comes straight from the Bible. Jesus said "If you love me, you will keep my commandments" (John 14:15). NASB

Think about it.

As a child, if you loved your parents you would want to do what they asked you to do—even if it wasn't exactly what you wanted to do at that point. If you love another person and they ask you to do something, you feel a certain joy and satisfaction in doing it for them even if in itself it isn't the most pleasant of tasks.

In the very same way, if we love God we will want to do what God asks us to do.

Yes, I know. It says keep God's commandments. But realistically, we don't have to do what God commands us to do. We can decide not to. So if we think of it as God asking us to do this and not to do that, then it's really the same as someone we love asking us to do something, or asking us not to do something that they don't like. It's true that sometimes—perhaps often—what God is commanding us to do is exactly what we don't want to do, and what God is commanding us not to do is precisely what we do which we become disobedience to the almighty God.

But if we truly want to love God with our whole heart, we will set our mind and our heart on doing what God wants us to do, and not doing what God doesn't want us to do, as we understand it our God is love and His love endures forever

2. We can love God by caring for the people God has made. This one also comes from the Bible. As part of the parable of the sheep and the goats, Jesus said:

Then the King will say to those at his right hand, "Come, you that are blessed by my Father, inherit the kingdom prepared for you from the foundation of the world; for I was hungry and you gave me food, I was thirsty and you gave me something to drink, I was a stranger and you welcomed me, I was naked and you gave me clothing, I was sick and you took care of me, I was in prison and you visited me." Then the righteous will answer him, "Lord, when was it that we saw you hungry and gave you food, or thirsty and gave you something to drink? And when was it that we saw you a stranger and welcomed you, or naked and gave you clothing? And when was it that we saw you sick or in prison and visited you?" And the king will answer them, "Truly I tell you, just as you did it for one of the least of these who are members of my family, you did it for me." (Matthew 25:34–40) NRSV

You see, God loves every single one of the people that God has created. God feels joy when even the least, most broken down of us feels some small bit of happiness, contentment, and love. Every time we do something for one of God's creatures—not only human, but also animal, plant, and even inanimate rocks and soil—we are doing it for God, and giving God joy. In a very real way, every small act of service, kindness, thoughtfulness, and caring that we do for someone else is an act of loving God.

That's why Jesus said that the second greatest commandment is like the first. When we love our neighbor as we love ourselves, we are also loving God with our whole heart, soul, and mind.

3. We can love God by feeling joy in the things God feels joy in.

Okay, let's admit it. Some of the things we feel joy in are not the sort of thing God feels joy in. For example, it's natural for us humans to feel pleasure when someone who has hurt us feels pain. We want to get back at them for what they did to us. We want them to feel the pain they have caused us to feel.

But that's not the sort of thing God feels joy in. When Jesus was on the cross, as he looked down at those who were causing him such great pain, what did he say? Did he curse them and wish a miserable death upon them?

Not at all. He said:

Father, forgive them, for they do not know what they are doing. (Luke 23:34) KJV

Earlier, Jesus had taught the people:

You have heard that it was said, "You shall love your neighbor and hate your enemy." But I say to you, Love your enemies and pray for those who persecute you, so that you may be children of your Father in heaven; for he makes his sun rise on the evil and on the good, and sends rain on the righteous and on the unrighteous. (Matthew 5:43–45) NRSV

And in the book of Ezekiel, God says to those who are flouting his laws and breaking his commandments:

I take no pleasure in the death of anyone, says the Lord God. Repent, then, and live! (Ezekiel 18:32) NIV

God takes no pleasure in the pain or the death of those who have made themselves into God's enemies by doing all sorts of evil and destructive things. Rather, God's desire is always for them to turn away from their evil and destructive ways so that they can experience true joy and happiness.

If we wish to love God with our whole heart, instead of wishing pain and death on those who have hurt us, we will wish and hope that they will realize and regret the wrongs they have done so that they can turn from them and begin to experience a life of happiness and joy. This is just one example of how loving God is feeling joy in the things God feels joy in. As we learn more and more about what God is like and what gives God joy, we can learn to feel joy in the same things God feels joy in. The more we do this, the more we will love God with our whole heart.

Why Not Trust God?

7 Daily Steps to Trust in the Lord with All Your Heart

Perhaps you've been told that as a Christian you must learn to "trust in the Lord with all your heart." But this famous passage from Proverbs 3 contains more than just a general statement about living. Instead, you'll find the steps you need each day to truly walk with God. Follow these 7 daily steps to make sure you're leaning on the Lord:

1. Don't Depend on You

We live in a world where trust must be earned and seems to be in short supply. But Solomon, the famous king who wrote Proverbs, knew that trust is exactly where we must start:

Trust in the LORD with all your heart and lean not on your own understanding (Proverbs 3:5) NIV

Most of us have faced disappointments, which have taught us that we can only depend upon ourselves. But living the life God has called us to means unlearning that lesson.

Instead, we're meant to rest in God's understanding. We may know in our minds that He possesses all wisdom:

"Oh, the depth of the riches of the wisdom and knowledge of God! How unsearchable his judgments, and his paths beyond tracing out!" (Romans 11:33) NIV

But sometimes trusting Him completely like that can be tough. So, each day we must consciously lay aside our own plans and expectations—and surrender to His plans. What if we don't feel like we can trust Him like that? That's where step 2 comes in…

2. **Cry out to God**

Surrendering to God begins with our lips and our thoughts. We need more than a commitment to depend on Him; we need to cry out to Him to show that dependence.

"In all your ways acknowledge him, and he will make your paths straight" (Proverbs 3:6) NIV

When we pray, we admit that His ways are higher than ours. We show that we're leaving our troubles and burdens and dreams in His capable hands. In fact, the Bible promises that when we reach out to Him in prayer, He hears us:

"Evening, morning, and noon I cry out in distress, and he hears my voice." (Psalm 55:17) NIV

We handed the keys of our lives to Him, and we know that He's able to lead us. But in order for that to work, we have to…

3. **Run from Evil**

So much in this world can clutter up our relationship with God. John, the writer of the fourth gospel, describes them as the desires of the flesh, the lusts of the eyes, and the pride in our lives (1 John 2:16). In other words, our blessings can easily become our stumbling blocks when we think of them as what we deserve or what we need to be happy. Instead, life works best when we remember the true source of our blessings—God—and focus on the things that please Him:

"Do not be wise in your own eyes; fear the LORD and shun evil." (Proverbs 3:7) NIV

Sometimes, the only way to live the life God wants us to live is by separating ourselves from the bad influences that keep dragging us down. That works the best when we start pursuing something else in their place:

"Flee the evil desires of youth, and pursue righteousness, faith, love, and peace, along with those who call on the Lord out of a pure heart." (2 Timothy 2:22) NIV

Is that easy? Not at all. Fleeing from the evil desires that pull at us means spending a lot of time crying out to God and leaning on Him. But our Creator promises to honor our commitment to Him when we shun evil:

"This will bring health to your body and nourishment to your bones." (Proverbs 3:8)

When we pursue Him, we find life—abundant life. Running from evil and pursuing God doesn't come naturally to most of us. Instead, it means we have to make a serious change.

4. **Put God First in Your Life**

It's easiest to put ourselves first. When something good happens, we want to congratulate ourselves with a reward. When something bad happens, we want to console ourselves or find someone to blame. In other words, we often have a "me-centric" starting place. And when it comes to money, the struggle is even harder. But Solomon, who had quite a bit of wealth himself, knew that his money didn't belong to him.

"Honor the LORD with your wealth, with the first fruits of all your crops; then your barns will be filled to overflowing, and your vats will brim over with new wine." (Proverbs 3:9–10) If we can trust God with the first of our wealth, we're truly showing how much we depend on Him. Handing over the first part of our paycheck takes a huge amount of faith, after all. But doing so means being God-centric.

To get there, though, make sure you...

5. Check Yourself by God's Word

Let's be honest. We aren't so good at evaluating ourselves. We will go to great lengths to excuse our behavior, our actions, and our sins. Who needs a defense attorney when we can pretty much find a reason for any bad thing we do? The prophet Jeremiah captures this very well:

"The heart is deceitful above all things and beyond cure. Who can understand it?" (Jeremiah 17:9) NIV

If we're ever going to truly trust in God and flee evil, we have to know exactly where we stand. We have to find an objective measure that tells us the truth. And that truth comes from God and His Word.

Of course, that doesn't mean we'll always like what we see or how we see it.

"My son, do not despise the LORD's discipline and do not resent his rebuke" (Proverbs 3:11) NIV

That's right. Sometimes it takes something bad happening or seeing ourselves in a bad light before we finally admit that we need to change. And the more we're in the Bible, the more likely this is to happen.

"I have hidden your word in my heart that I might not sin against you." (Psalm 119:11) NIV

When we have Scripture planted firmly in our hearts, God will often use that to deal with us.

6. **Listen to the Holy Spirit**

When Jesus promised to send the Holy Spirit to the church, He told His disciples that this Counselor would be their spiritual compass or GPS:

"But the Counselor, the Holy Spirit, whom the Father will send in my name, will teach you all things and will remind you of everything I have said to you." (John 14:26) NIV

As we go through our day, this same Holy Spirit guides us, too. That means we don't have to go it alone or hope we're getting it right. No, the Holy Spirit leads us into all truth and protects us:

"Guard the good deposit that was entrusted to you—guard it with the help of the Holy Spirit who lives in us." (2 Timothy 1:14) After all, the gift of the Holy Spirit to us believers reminds us that we can truly...

7. **Rest in God's Love**

When we face a difficult world each day, we can sometimes wonder if God even cares. Why do bad things happen? Where is God when I need Him? Solomon reminds us that God never takes a break or leaves us to fend for ourselves: "because the LORD disciplines those he loves, as a father the son he delights in." (Proverbs 3:12) Even in the midst of turmoil, God sticks with us and uses those challenges to shape us. When we understand that, our perspective completely flips. No longer do we see our setbacks as failures; we see them as moments when God, as our loving Father, works on us. And that's exactly why we can trust in the Lord with all our hearts. He cares for us each and every day. He gives us what we need to thrive. He pours blessing after blessing upon us.

Of course, following each of these daily steps isn't easy. That's why Jesus said we have to deny ourselves and follow Him (Matthew 16:24). Trusting God takes a whole-hearted commitment from dawn till dusk. But we're never alone in it.

"And surely I am with you always, to the very end of the age." (Matthew 28:20b) NIV

CHAPTER EIGHT

SHAPED THROUGH TOUGH TIMES

In your walk with God and your service to God, you will encounter certain challenges. This is a normal part of the Christian walk, with Jesus Christ warning us that these things will come our way. They are to be expected. Even Paul, in the book of Acts, was warned by a prophet that when he goes to Jerusalem he will be persecuted. Despite the pleas from some brethren for him not to go, Paul was steadfast in his resolve to go because he had to preach Christ. Read the full account in Acts 21:10–15.

Paul suffered many things at the hands of both Jews and Gentiles, and through it all, he was even encouraging people the more. He knew that "the testing of our faith produces patience, which builds our experience and that experience revitalizes our hope. And hope does not put us to shame". [Paraphrased from Rom. 5:3–5] Let us look at some of the things that trials can do in our lives, when we approach it with the right attitude.

- **Tribulation tests our identity as Christians.**

Tribulation tests our identity. In the parable of the sower (Matthew 13:1-23), Jesus described several situations. The seed that landed on rocky places did not have much soil. It sprang up quickly, because the soil was shallow. When the sun came up, the plants were scorched, and they withered because they had no root. Jesus said that the one who received the seed that fell on rocky places is the man who hears the word and at once receives it with joy. Since he has no root, he lasts only a short time. When trouble or persecutions come because of the Word, he quickly falls away. The one who received the seed that fell among thorns is the man who hears the word, but the worries of this life and the deceitfulness of wealth choke it, making it unfruitful. The seed that fell on good soil produced a good crop. By implication, that seed that fell on good soil stayed connected to the source of its life and was not destroyed by trouble, persecution, the worries of this life, or the deceitfulness of wealth. When we deal with tribulation as we should, it authenticates our true identity as believers.

- **Tribulation tests our faith**

"These [trials] have come so that your faith of greater worth than gold, which perishes even though refined by fire may be proved genuine and may result in praise, glory and honor when Jesus Christ is revealed" (1 Peter 1:7).

- **Tribulation tests our sense of purpose.**

When I was in my first year of medical school, I was about one minute late to histology class two or three times in a row. Our professor approached me in the laboratory and notified me that my tardiness reflected on my "sense of purpose." I was never late again, because I realized how it would reflect on my character. As it says in James, "Blessed is the man who perseveres under trial, because when he has stood the test, he will receive the crown of life that God has promised to those who love him"(James 1:2).

• Tribulation tests our obedience

"The reason I wrote you was to see if you would stand the test and be obedient in everything" (2 Corinthians 2:9). We are tested to teach us to rely on God.

"We do not want you to be uninformed, brothers, about the hardships we suffered in the province of Asia. We were under great pressure, far beyond our ability to endure, so that we despaired even of life. Indeed, in our hearts we felt the sentence of death. But this happened that we might not rely on ourselves but on God, who raises the dead. He has delivered us from such a deadly peril, and he will deliver us. On him we have set our hope that he will continue to deliver us, as you help us by your prayers. Then many will give thanks on our behalf for the gracious favor granted us in answer to the prayers of many" (2 Corinthians 1:8-11). NIV

• We are tested so that it will go well with us

"He gave you manna to eat in the desert, something your fathers had never known, to humble and to test you so that in the end it might go well with you" (Deuteronomy 8:16).

Some people do not pass the test In the New Testament. There is a Greek word, adokimos, that speaks of people who are tested but do not pass the test. It is used several times in the New Testament. I have included selected quotations:

"No, I beat my body and make it my slave so that after I have preached to others, I myself will not be disqualified for the prize" (1 Corinthians 9:27). NIV

"Examine yourselves to see whether you are in the faith; test yourselves. Do you not realize that Christ Jesus is in you unless of course you fail the test? And I trust that you will discover that we have not failed the test. Now we pray to God that you will not do anything wrong" (2 Corinthians 13:5-7a). NIV

"They claim to know God, but by their actions they deny him. They are detestable, disobedient and unfit for doing anything good" (Titus 1:16). NIV

"But land that produces thorns and thistles is worthless and is in danger of being cursed. In the end it will be burned" (Hebrews 6:8). NIV

Consider what you know about God's saving grace and love, and examine whether you are in a situation because you can find a way to glorify God through it. Let the tests and trials you go through provide an avenue for you to serve God even more. Let people see your love for God, amidst adversity and let them be inspired to serve God even when things seem bleak. Remember, joy is a command.

CHAPTER NINE

STAY COMMITTED TO YOUR CHRISTIAN FAITH

It's sad that many Christians struggle with their Christian life and don't know what to do. Some people just need simple steps on how to stay focused on God in the busy and distracting world we live in. Backsliding is often subtle. This is why every Christian needs to regularly use the following steps to make sure they are avoiding the subtle and dangerous backsliding from their Christian faith. Remember that God is always with you no matter how many times you backslide, but you must keep your part too

1. **Examine your faith and Christian life regularly.**

Examine yourselves to see whether you are in the faith; test yourselves. Do you not realize that Christ Jesus is in you—unless, of course, you fail the test? 2 Corinthians 13:5 (NIV) You wouldn't go that long without checking your oil level and other fluids in your car, so why would you leave your spiritual life unchecked?

2. **Turn back right away if you find yourself drifting away.**

Read the Bible to remember God's faith and love, and to remember what He did for us. See to it, brothers, that none of you has a sinful, unbelieving heart that turns away from the living God. But encourage one another daily, as long as it is called Today, so that none of you may be hardened by sin's deceitfulness. Hebrews 3:12-13 (NIV) Just like driving, you will know when you are drifting because things will be different when you pass the right or left barrier. You will have warning signs like coldness toward spiritual things, irritability, less Bible reading, and similar things. You must do step one in order to know you need to do step two.

3. **Come to God daily for forgiveness and the cleansing of sins.**

If we confess our sins, he is faithful and just and will forgive us our sins and purify us from all unrighteousness. 1 John 1:9 (NIV). Blessed are those who wash their robes, that they may have the right to the tree of life and may go through the gates into the city. Revelation 22:14 (NIV).

Repent of a sin you commit and make sure to not do it again. If thoughts of guilt come to you trying to make you think you are not forgiven, just simply ignore them and know that God has forgiven you. As long as you are struggling with sin, that means you are trying to resist the sin.

4. **Seek the Lord with all your heart daily.**

And you, my son Solomon, acknowledge the God of your father, and serve him with wholehearted devotion and with a willing mind, for the Lord searches every heart and understands every motive behind the thoughts. If you seek him, he will be found by you; but if you forsake him, he will reject you forever. I Chronicles 28:9 (NIV) Read your bible and pray daily. Set your heart on God and he will gradually reveal himself to you. He will not ignore a truly repentant, honest, and persistent person seeking Him.

5. **Stay in the word and keep studying and learning every day.**

Hold on to instruction, do not let it go; guard it well, for it is your life. Proverbs 4:13 (NIV)

Make a habit of reading the word of God. At first it may be hard or you may face distractions, but make an effort to make it a habit. Once you make yourself do it regularly, you will eventually grow into liking it and the word will become alive to you.

6. **Stay in fellowship with other believers.**

The Christian life is not to be lived alone but with others so they can strengthen you in hard times.

And let us not neglect our meeting together, as some people do, but encourage and warn each other, especially now that the day of his coming back again is drawing near. Hebrews 10:25 (NLT). Simply going to church and seeing others who are wanting to know God will help you seek God more easily. Church is a good way to make friends too.

7. **Stay strong in your faith. Expect difficult times in your Christian life.**

All men will hate you because of me, but he who stands firm to the end will be saved. Matthew 10:22 (NIV).

It is for freedom that Christ has set us free. Stand firm, then, and do not let yourselves be burdened again by a yoke of slavery. Galatians 5:1 (NIV).

You will struggle, but don't give in. Remember, "no pain, no gain". If you aren't struggling, you are probably not doing something you should be doing. The devil doesn't want you to be a Christian and if you aren't butting heads with the devil, you are probably going in the same direction he is.

8. **Persevere, persevere, persevere.**

Be diligent in these matters; give yourself wholly to them, so that everyone may see your progress. Watch your life and doctrine closely. Persevere in them, because if you do, you will save both yourself and your hearers. 1 Timothy 4:15-17 (NIV).

Stand your ground. Realize that you cannot fail, because if you do, you won't make it to heaven. There really is no option. Heaven or hell, it's up to you. To go to heaven, you will have to work, fight, take pain, insults, and setbacks in your life, and do things you won't necessarily enjoy.

9. **Run this race of life to win**.

Do you not know that in a race all the runners run, but only one gets the prize? Run in such a way as to get the prize. Everyone who competes in the games goes into strict training... we do it to get a crown that will last forever. 1 Corinthians 9: 24-25 (NIV) I have fought the good fight, I have finished the race, I have kept the faith. Now there is in store for me the crown of righteousness... 2 Timothy 4:7-8 (NIV) Stay your course. You are not just running this race for a crown; you are running this race to find true meaning and purpose once this life is over. Once you die, it's over. All you can take with you is your soul and your good deeds and what you did for the Lord. All your degrees, awards, houses, cars, hobbies, and more will be gone forever. Fear not, because you will have new and better and eternal versions of all these things in heaven. All you have to do is make sure you get there.

10. **Remind yourself of past victories.**

Remember those earlier days after you had received the light, when you stood your ground in a great contest in the face of suffering. So do not throw away your confidence; it will be richly rewarded. You need to persevere so that when you have done the will of God, you will receive what he has promised ... we are not of those who shrink back and are destroyed, but of those who believe and are saved. Hebrews 10: 32, 35-39 (NIV)

One tactic the enemy loves using is to remind you of your present situation and get you to forget what the Lord has protected you from, saved you from, and provided you with. You are a walking miracle and you don't even realize it. God has great plans for you in the future too.

CHAPTER TEN

BENEFITS OF SERVING GOD

Serving God wholeheartedly brings a plethora of benefits. They are immeasurable and they are overwhelming. Should you have these benefits for serving God, life is going to be heaven on earth. The Scripture below stipulates the benefits of the life that has diligently served God.

Psa 103:1-22 KJV

Bless the LORD, O my soul: and all that is within me, bless his holy name.

Bless the LORD, O my soul, and forget not all his benefits:

*Who **forgiveth** all thine iniquities; who **healeth** all thy diseases;*

*Who **redeemeth** thy life from destruction; who **crowneth** thee with lovingkindness and tender mercies;*

*Who **satisfieth** thy mouth with good things; so that thy youth is renewed like the eagle's.*

The Scripture contains all the benefits there is to enjoy. Greater grace is available for us as Christian and that is joyous to know. Apparently, one of the scriptures that brings relief to one's spirit is the one above. This is knowing that my God will sure reward our service to Him. It is a celebration of the goodness and blessings of God. It contains no supplication, no request, no petition or plea. It is pure unadulterated praise to God. David was awestruck with God's blessings!

When we read Psalm 103, we need to hear the Holy Spirit speaking personally to us. He is telling us to get with the Kingdom program of praise to God!

OUR DAILY FOCUS

- **To cultivate an attitude of praise and thankfulness to God. (103:1-2a)**

In the opening two verses of this psalm, David repeats twice the self-focused exhortation to "bless the LORD." The term "bless," when used in reference to God, is to recognize and declare that God is the source of all that is good. It includes delight of heart and gratitude for all He is and all He does. The word "LORD" (translated from **Jehovah**) is God's personal name and, since the giving of the Law at Mt Sinai, serves to remind us that God enters into covenant relationship with His people. In other words, He is a God who cares about every aspect of our lives and desires to encourage, comfort, and provide for all our needs. This self-exhortation to bless the LORD is not unique to this psalm, for example,

"I will bless the LORD at all times; His praise shall continually be in my mouth" (Psa. 34:1 KJV).

The verbal phrase "I will bless the LORD," is not a simple future tense ("I will bless the LORD sometime"), or even a statement of fact ("I will bless the LORD"). It is a polite way of commanding oneself to take action! In other words, don't just think about it, or mentally agree with the need to bless the LORD, but take a firm grip upon yourself and immediately initiate the required action.

How important is praise and thanksgiving in the life of a believer? The Psalmist tells us, "From the rising of the sun to its setting, the name of the LORD is to be praised!" (Psalm 113:3 KJV). In agrarian societies, without the blessing of electricity, people usually began their day with the rising of the sun and ended it and began preparing for bed shortly after it set.

This means that we are to cultivate an attitude of praise and thankfulness to God all day long! Again, the psalmist wrote, "Not to us, O LORD, not to us, but to your name give glory, for the sake of your steadfast love and your faithfulness!" (115:1). Then he resolves, "We will bless the LORD from this time forth and forever more. Praise the LORD!" (115:18).

The last three verses of Psalm 103 contain exhortations for everyone and everything to praise God. "Bless the LORD, O you his angels, you mighty ones who do his word, obeying the voice of his word! Bless the LORD, all his hosts, his ministers, who do his will! Bless the LORD, all his works, in all places of his dominion. Bless the LORD, O my soul!" (vs. 20-23) Notice that the psalmist realizes that the cultivation of an attitude of praise and thankfulness to God must begin within his own heart. May I pause at this point and ask you, dear reader, are you responding to God's call to cultivate a daily focus of praise and thanksgiving? Let's begin right now!

- **Count your blessings and don't forget them. (103:2)**

In addition to cultivating an attitude of praise and thankfulness to God, we should also count our blessings and make sure we don't forget them. The psalmist said,

"Bless the LORD, O my soul, and forget not all his benefits!" (103:2). KJV

Human beings are forgetful creatures. It is amazing to see how many times the Scriptures warn us about "forgetting" (see Deut. 4:9,23; 6:12; 8:11,14, 19; 9:7; 25:19; 2 Kings 17:38; Psa. 9:17; 50:22; 78:7; Pro. 3:1; 4:5; Hos 4:6). For most of us, it would be beneficial to keep a record of all the answers to prayer and the blessings God brings into our lives. It would help us to remember. The psalmist asked, "What shall I render unto GOD for all his benefits toward me?"

There Are Wonderful Benefits That We Inherit

Make a joyful noise to the Lord, all the earth! Serve the Lord with gladness!" Psalm 100:1&2

Sometimes I just get so amazed. People will say, "I don't think you should be talking about the pursuit of joy. I think you should be talking about serving Jesus and obeying Jesus."

I say, "What Bible do you read?" "Serve the Lord with gladness!" Serve the Lord with gladness! This is not rocket science. This is clear! Serve the Lord with gladness! There is a kind of service he doesn't like: murmuring service, bored service, and glum service. Serve the Lord with gladness. This is biblical! Are we a biblical people, or do we just get our truths from our emotions or non-emotions?

Psalm 32:11, "Be glad in the Lord, and rejoice, O righteous, and shout for joy, all you upright in heart!" Psalm 37:4, "Delight yourself in the Lord, and he will give you the desires of your heart." That's a command, not a suggestion. It's not, "If you don't want to delight in me, that's okay. Go ahead with your house or whatever." It's not an option. It's a command.

"Joy is not an option. It's a command."

Philippians 4:4 ESV, "Rejoice in the Lord always; again I will say, rejoice." Paul was writing from prison. I want to make sure you hear me say that Paul, when he writes like that — "Rejoice in the Lord always; again I will say, rejoice" — this man knew more suffering than all of you combined, probably.

I'll read you one of the lists of his suffering. 2 Corinthians 6:4–5: "As servants of God we commend ourselves in every way: by great endurance, in afflictions, hardships, calamities, beatings..." If you were beaten for Jesus, I would like to know who you are. Come up and tell me, "I was beaten for Jesus," and I will bow down and give thanks for you and your faith.

Continuing in 2 Corinthians 6, ". . . calamities, beatings, imprisonments, riots, labors, sleepless nights, hunger; . . . through honor and dishonor, through slander and praise. We are treated as impostors, and yet are true; as unknown, and yet well known; as dying, and behold, we live; as punished, and yet not killed" — and here's the key phrase for me — "as sorrowful, yet always rejoicing."

Isn't that amazing? If there was no hint of despair or discouragement after that list — and that's the short list, the long one's in chapter 11; that's the short list of his pain — and he said, "sorrowful, yet always rejoicing", I think we can take assurance in the fact that the same God who kept Paul and gave him comfort, will also keep us and give us comfort.

I want you to be able to taste that. I want suffering people to read this book, be encouraged, know that God has got them in His hands, and feel like they can continue in this life with the help of God. Don't think that we are not chipper people who have never tasted the dark night of the soul, never tasted the loss of a loved one, and never tasted the love of a wayward child. "These people are so naïve about reality they just jabber about joy", that's what you may think. I don't want that. The opposite of joy is not suffering. It's despair in suffering. I personally have gone through periods of great struggle, but some of the things the Lord showed me, which I am sharing with you, kept me going even in my moments of difficulty.

CHAPTER ELEVEN

JUST HOW FAR?

How far are we willing to go for God? In Matthew 5:29-30, Christ said that if anything gets in the way of doing God's work, then we have to conquer it. We have to cut things off, if necessary—take drastic action. We can't allow those problems to slow us down because if they do, it will slow down God's work.

In Luke 14, Christ gives a parable in which a master of a house prepared a royal feast for an exclusive gathering (verses 16-17). When the invitations were sent out, however, the people turned them down. The people made excuses because of the strong attachments they had in the world (verses 18-20).

In response, the master told his servant, "Go out quickly into the streets and lanes of the city, and bring in hither the poor, and the maimed, and the halt, and the blind" (verse 21). In other words, go out and find those who are willing to give up those things in order to dwell with God.

"And the servant said, Lord, it is done as thou hast commanded, and yet there is room. And the lord said unto the servant, Go out into the highways and hedges, and compel them to come in, that my house may be filled. For I say unto you, that none of those men which were bidden shall taste of my supper" (verses 22-24 KJV).Those who

were invited originally end up getting shut out entirely because of their many lame excuses.

The lesson of this parable, Christ said, is in the commitment to follow Him: "If any man come to me, and hate not his father, and mother, and wife, and children, and brethren, and sisters, yea, and his own life also, he cannot be my disciple" (verse 26). If we commit to follow God, we are saying we are willing to give it all up for God—even our own lives, if necessary. God's Family and God's work must come first—ahead of our own flesh and blood; ahead of material things or pursuits.

Understand just how serious this commitment really is. This is not some puny endeavor: It's the work of God. We ought to be fully committed and devoted to God, even if we do not have the zeal or encouragement to do so. We have to follow and trust God completely even in the midst of adversity, knowing that He will give us the grace for devotion and reward our efforts.

One man who was seriously committed to God was Joshua. The Bible says he and Caleb "wholly followed" God (Joshua 14:6-8 KJV). In response, Moses told them, *"Surely the land whereon thy feet have trodden shall be thine inheritance, and thy children's forever, because thou hast wholly followed the Lord my God" (verse 9).*

Here is one characteristic that helped shape Joshua's courageous nature: He served God with his whole heart. God's way of life is to go forward, sincerely, wholeheartedly and earnestly, as far as you can go in the direction of His law. The Christian life is a life of growing and improving in character—of overcoming—of becoming more and more like Christ. If we are not growing, we are dying.

In Matthew 5, Jesus Christ magnifies the law given in the Old Testament. In a sense, He is saying, "I know you are well aware of all the human customs and traditions of the day. But I'm talking to you Christians about elevating the standard far above that" (verses 38-39). In verse 48 He challenges His disciples to "[become] ye therefore perfect, even as your Father which is in heaven is perfect." What a standard!

This scripture encapsulates the gospel of God. It is all about human beings actually becoming like God Himself. God is a perfectionist. How much of a perfectionist are you? We should develop a desire for perfection in everything that we do.

As true Christians, we are called upon to do more than is required of us—to be a living sacrifice (Romans 12:1-2). Colossians 3:23 says, "And whatsoever ye do, do it heartily, as to the Lord, and not unto men." (See also Ecclesiastes 9:10.) God expects total commitment from us. This is not easy.

On Feb. 25, 1955, Herbert W. Armstrong wrote, "God has never intended our lives, yielded to Him for His service, to be a proverbial soft 'bed of roses.' God has not intended our Christian lives in His service to run smooth and easy, with no problems, no concerns. God intended—ordained—that we should be confronted with continual problems, difficulties, troubles—that we should have to make constant sacrifices, learning to give up our own ways and wants—even some of our money, and the things we want to buy with it!"

Christ said in Matthew 16:24-27, "If any man will come after me, let him deny himself, and take up his cross, and follow me. For whosoever will save his life shall lose it: and whosoever will lose his life for my sake shall find it. ... For the Son of man shall come in the glory of his Father with his angels; and then he shall reward every man according to his works."

If we hold back, we might lose out entirely. The way to gain eternal life and a reward in God's Kingdom is to give up our life right now—to lay it down, and sacrifice it for God's work!

Strive to put your whole heart into God's work. Don't be a half-hearted Christian. Don't give in to the downward pull of human nature to be spiritually lazy. Set your mind and your will to obey God with all your heart.

Real spiritual growth comes when you are totally wrapped up in God's work. God's work is a work of giving, serving and helping others. It is a work that requires sacrifice. It is a work of love. It is a work worth fighting, suffering and dying for! If you will commit yourself and give up your life for this work, Jesus Christ says you will gain eternal life.

1. **Serving God in sincerity and truth.**

Joshua 24: 13-15(NKJV)

John 4:24 (NKJV). Serving God wholeheartedly means serving God in Spirit and in truth. When you are given a responsibility, do not grumble for when you grumble you water down the blessing God has earmarked for you. It is also important that you do not serve God blindly. Let your personality both mentally and spiritually be in church to serve Him.

Reminiscent of a child learning the numerals, when he knows how to count from 1-50, he is excited but you do not ask him to stop there just because he has learnt a few. Rather, you encourage him to go all the way. It is in this manner that we are expected to serve GOD. You move from one stage to the other.

2. **Serving God boldly.**

Daniel 3:16 (MSG)

Be bold in your service to God. Do not get shy when you are about to preach the gospel. Serving God boldly is best illustrated by the three Hebrew children in the days of Babylon.

Daniel 3:16-18 MSG– Shadrach, Meshach, and Abednego answered King Nebuchadnezzar, "Your threat means nothing to us. If you throw us in the fire, the God we serve can rescue us from your roaring furnace and anything else you might cook up, O king. But even if he doesn't, it wouldn't make a bit of difference, O king. We still wouldn't serve your gods or worship the gold statue you set up."

3. **Serving in the pattern of Godliness.**

2 Timothy 1:3, 13, Romans 15:4

This encompasses learning from the testimonies of our fathers in faith. Lessons should be learnt from illustrations and examples set by our senior pastors and our resident pastors who do admonish us on commitment in our service to God. We shouldn't hear all these as gist, but we should learn from them and ensure we do better than they did in our dedication to the work of God.

4. **Serving God consistently.**

We should learn to serve God regardless of the trials and tribulations we might be facing at point in time in our Christian walk with Christ. Serving God in the most difficult circumstances and situations, including those times when you pray and don't get answers.

Luke 2: 37, Revelations 7:12, 15-16

When you serve God wholeheartedly there are blessings attached-Col 3:24(NKJV). Ensure you serve God with the whole of your heart for there is a grace for wholehearted service.

Prophetic Declarations

Receive the grace to serve God wholeheartedly. Receive lands you did not labour for in the name of Jesus! Receive cities you did not build; they are becoming yours in the name of Jesus! What you lack most you will have most in the name of Jesus! Amen.

CONCLUSION

God Smiles When We Obey

"Just tell me what to do and I will do it, Lord. As long as I live I'll wholeheartedly obey." Psalm 119:33 (LB)

Often we try to offer God partial obedience. We want to pick and choose the commands we obey.

God smiles when we obey him wholeheartedly. That means doing whatever God asks without reservation or hesitation. You don't procrastinate and say, "I'll pray about it." You do it without delay. Every parent knows that delayed obedience is really disobedience. God doesn't owe you an explanation or reason for everything he asks you to do. Understanding can wait, but obedience can't. Instant obedience will teach you more about God than a lifetime of Bible discussions. In fact, you will never understand some commands until you obey them first. Obedience unlocks understanding.

Often we try to offer God partial obedience. We want to pick and choose the commands we obey. We make a list of the commands we like and obey those while ignoring the ones we think are unreasonable, difficult, expensive, or unpopular. I'll attend church but I won't tithe. I'll read my Bible but won't forgive the person who hurt me. Yet partial obedience is disobedience. Wholehearted obedience is done joyfully, with enthusiasm. The Bible says, "Obey him gladly." (Psalm 100:2 LB)

This is the attitude of David: "Just tell me what to do and I will do it, Lord. As long as I live I'll wholeheartedly obey." (Psalm 119:33 LB) James, speaking to Christians, said, "We please God by what we do and not only by what we believe." (James 2:24 CEV)

God's Word is clear that you can't earn your salvation. It comes only by grace, not your effort. But as a child of God you can bring pleasure to your heavenly Father through obedience. Any act of obedience is also an act of worship.

Why is obedience so pleasing to God? Because it proves you really love him. Jesus said, "If you love me, you will obey my commandments." (John 14:15 TEV)

So, beloved, in times of trouble and seemingly difficult circumstances, keep on holding on to God and serving him wholeheartedly. Serve with all your heart, with all your mind and with all your strength, and be assured that God will reward your labor of love.

ABOUT THE AUTHOR

Betty Prempeh-Twimasi is a dynamic and energetic woman of God with an Apostolic mandate and a passion to see the body of Christ come into their full potential in their service to God. She is a motivational speaker, an Evangelist, Teacher, Revivalist, Intercessor, Administrator, Caterer, a marriage counselor and a minister who is highly interested in seeing Christian marriages flourish in today's society. This is evidenced in the various programs she hosts such as the Marriage Survival Program, and Family Empowerment through Ministers & Church Workers' Conference and also coaches Couples, Singles, Widows, and Single Parents throughout the world.

She has preached all over the world in countries like Italy, Germany, Nigeria, Ghana, England. Scotland, Belguim, Togo, Cote D'lvoire Holland and other countries. She also owns a Radio Station called Compassion Radio where she hosts a program through which she reaches many and preaches the gospel of salvation. She counsels in many international churches throughout the world and has a missionary ministry called The Lord Compassion Outreach International which is helping the needy who have lost their families. As a Mother and also a wife she makes sure she does all to glorify the name of the Lord

Reverend Prempeh-Twimasi received a Degree in Biblical Studies and Theology at Southeastern Baptist Theological Seminary (SEBTS) and a Degree in Theology at Gate of

Heaven Seminary. She has a Bachelor's Degree in Catering, and from the School of Evangelical Associates, a degree in Administration. She became a certified nursing assistant; a profession which she engaged in for roughly 10 years. A series of events saw her answer to a long sounding call from God, and after she answered that call, she has not turned back. She is currently part of a pastoral team at the Resurrection Power and Living Bread Ministry in the U.S. A. and runs, the Compassion Ministry which is concerned with spreading the love of God through donations, giving and helping the needy.

She has been married to Mr John Domfel Twimasi for the past 18 years and is blessed with three Beautiful children: Fredirck, Chelsea, and Ebenezer Prempeh Twimasi

Reverend Betty Prempeh-Twimasi has an unwavering assurance in the power of God, and in His faithfulness to see her through difficult circumstances and encourages all people she comes across to remain faithful to the call of God upon their lives. She has gone through pains in sickness and also throughout her calling but nothing stops her from achieving her goals and also accomplish the greatness of the Lord. Let us stand for the Lord for the days are evil and the Time is near. Amen and God bless you!

Printed in the United States
By Bookmasters